Marian Apparitions in the Catholic Church

An Overview

By Marilynn Hughes

The Out-of-Body Travel Foundation!

http://outofbodytravel.org

Our Lady of the Roses

2

All credits for quotations are included in the Bibliography.
For information, write to:

The Out-of-Body Travel Foundation!

http://outofbodytravel.org

MarilynnHughes@outofbodytravel.org

If this book is unavailable from your local bookseller, it may be obtained directly from the Out-of-Body Travel Foundation by going to www.outofbodytravel.org.

Having worked primarily in radio broadcasting, Marilynn Hughes spent several years as a news reporter, producer and anchor before deciding to stay at home with her three children. She's experienced, researched, written, and taught about out-of-body travel since 1987.

Books by Marilynn Hughes:
Come to Wisdom's Door
How to Have an Out-of-Body Experience!

The Mysteries of the Redemption
A Treatise on **Out-of-Body Travel** *and* **Mysticism**

The Mysteries of the Redemption Series in Five Volumes
(Same Book - Choose Your Format!)
Prelude to a Dream
Passage to the Ancient
Medicine Woman Within a Dream
Absolute Dissolution of Body and Mind
The Mystical Jesus

GALACTICA
A Treatise on **Death, Dying** *and the* **Afterlife**

THE PALACE OF ANCIENT KNOWLEDGE
A Treatise on **Ancient Mysteries**

Touched by the Nails
(Watch and Wait)
A Karmic Journey Revealed!

PRINCIPLES OF THE WORLD BEYOND DEATH

Michael Jackson:
The Afterlife Experiences
A Theology of Michael Jackson's Life and Lyrics

Near Death and Out-of-Body Experiences
(Auspicious Births and Deaths)
Of the Prophets, Saints, Mystics and Sages in World Religions

The Voice of the Prophets
Wisdom of the Ages - Volumes 1 - 12

At the Feet of the Masters

Miraculous Images:
Photographs Containing God's Fingerprints

Suffering:
The Fruits of Utter Desolation

We are all Shadows

The Overview Series
The Oral Transmissions of the 52 Soto Zen Buddhist Ancestors
The Doctors of the Catholic Church
The General Councils of the Catholic Church
Marian Apparitions in the Catholic Church
Heresies in the Catholic Church

Miraculous Phenomena in the Catholic Church
Fascinating Figures in World Religion
Practices, Prayer, Ritual, Liturgy, Sacraments and Theology in the
Catholic Church

Mystic Knowledge Series:

Out-of-Body Travel
Ghosts and Lost Souls
Spirit Guides and Guardian Angels
Reincarnation and Karma
Spiritual Warfare, Angels and Demons
Death, Dying and the Afterlife
Heaven, Hell and Purgatory
ExtraTerrestrials
Destiny and Prophecy
Initiations into the Mysteries
Visions of Jesus and the Saints
Ascension
Suffering and Sickness
Mystical Poetry

CHILDREN'S BOOKS

Teaching Stories of the Prophets in World Religions for Young People!
(Ages 10 to Adult)

World Religions and their Prophets for Little Children!
(Ages 2 - 8)

The Former Angel! - *A Children's Tale*
(Ages 2 - 8)

The Mystery of the Key to Heaven!
(Ages 2 - 10)

Streams in the Willow

The Story of One Family's Transformation from Original Sin

5

COMPILATIONS
Out-of-Body Travel and Near Death Experiences:
Compiled Works through 2006

World Religions and Ancient Sacred Texts: Compiled
Compiled Works through 2006

The Voice of the Prophets:
Abridged Lesser Known Texts

The Out-of-Body Travel Foundation Journals

Journal One: The Importance of the Seven Virtues and Vices in Understanding the Practice of Out-of-Body Travel!
Journal Two: My Out-of-Body Journey with Sai Baba, Hindu Avatar!
Journal Three: The History of 'The Out-of-Body Travel Foundation!'
Journal Four: A Menage of Wonderful Writers and Artists!
Journal Five: The Stories of Cherokee Elder, Willy Whitefeather!
Journal Six: Discerning your Vocation in Life by Learning the Difference Between Knowledge and Knowing!
Journal Seven: When Tragedy StrikesJournal Eight: Comparing the Buddhist Avalokiteswara's Descent into Hell with that of Jesus Christ!
Journal Nine: Huzur Maharaj Sawan Singh - Sant Mat (Sikh) Master Guru and Grandson Maharaj Charan Singh - Sant Mat (Sikh) Master Guru
Journal Ten: The Great Beyond
Journal Eleven: Ghosts and Lost Souls: Our Responsibility
Journal Twelve: The 800th Anniversary of Jalalludin Rumi, and the True Spiritual Heritage of Afghanistan and the Middle East
Journal Thirteen: Pensatia – Forgotten Rosicrucian Mystic
Journal Fourteen: Reverend John Macgowan – Forgotten Protestant Mystic
Journal Fifteen: A. Farnese – Forgotten Mystic Amanuensis (to Franchezzo)
Journal Sixteen: Comte St. Germain – Forgotten Immortal Mystic of the Mystery Schools
Journal Seventeen: Franz Hartmann – Forgotten Mystical Adept
Journal Eighteen: SA'D UD DIN MAHMŪD SHABISTARĪ –Forgotten Islamic Sufi Mystic
Journal Nineteen: Dionysius - Forgotten Christian Mystic of the Early Church
Issue Twenty: Acvaghosha - Forgotten Buddhist Mystic of the Mahayana Path
Issue Twenty One: Bishop Shelemon of Armenia – Forgotten Nestorian Christian Mystic
Issue Twenty Two: Abú Sa'íd Ibn Abi 'l-Khayr– Forgotten Islamic Mystic
Issue Twenty Three: Rev. G. Vale Owen - Forgotten Christian Mystic
Issue Twenty Four: Swami Abhedânanda- Forgotten Hindu Mystic
Issue Twenty Five: Moses Maimonides - Forgotten Jewish Mystic
Issue Twenty Six: The Bab - Forgotten Baha'i Mystic
Issue Twenty Seven: Shinran Shonin – Forgotten Mystic of Pure Land Buddhism

Issue Twenty Eight: Bustan of Sadi – Forgotten Persian Islamic Mystic
Issue Twenty Nine: John Bunyan – Forgotten Protestant Christian Mystic
Issue Thirty: Ixtlilxochitl and Nezahualcoyotl – Forgotten Aztec Mystics and Myth Bearers

Mystics Magazine

Issue One – Christian Mystical Theology, Conversations with Jacob Boehme
Issue Two - Buddhist Mystical Theology, Conversations with Charaka and Acvagosha
Issue Three – Islamic Mystical Theology, Conversations with Imam Ghazzali
Issue Four – Egyptian Mystical Theology, Conversations with W. Marsham Adams
Issue Five – Hindu Mystical Theology, Conversations with Sri Ramakrishna
Issue Six – Jewish Mystical Theology, Conversations with Rabbi Simeon
Issue Seven – Sikh Mystical Theology, Conversations with Guru Nanak
Issue Eight – Zoroastrian Mystical Theology, Conversations with Charles William King
Issue Nine – Bahai Mystical Theology, Conversations with Bahaullah

Go to our Web-Site:
The Out-of-Body Travel Foundation!
http://outofbodytravel.org

Marian Apparitions in the Catholic Church

An Overview

By Marilynn Hughes

CONTENTS

Our Lady of Akita, Japan – 8
Our Lady of America - 11
Our Lady of Banneux – 14
Our Lady of Beauraing - 17
Our Lady of Conyers, GA - 20
Our Lady of Czestochowa – 23
Our Lady of Fatima – 26
Our Lady of Garabandal – 29
Our Lady of Good Counsel – 32
Our Lady of Guadalupe – 35
Our Lady of La Salette – 38
Our Lady of Hungary – 40
Our Lady of Lourdes – 43
Our Lady of Medjugorje – 46
Our Lady of Mount Carmel – 49
Our Lady of Pellavoisin – 52
Our Lady of Pontmain – 55
Our Lady of Reconciliation – 58
Our Lady of Soufanieh – 61
Our Lady of the Americas – 64
Our Lady of the Miraculous Medal – 67
Our Lady of the Pillar – 70
Our Lady of the Rosary – 72
Our Lady of the Roses – 75
Our Lady of Zeitoun, Egypt – 78
Rosa Mystica - 81

Our Lady of Akita, Japan

The Blessed Virgin Manifesting through a Statue of
Mary

Sr. Agnes Sasagawa began what would become a
series of eight year apparitions when she received
three revelations in 1973 regarding future
chastisements.

In 1984, the Bishop of Niigata, bishop John Shojiro Ito,
wrote a letter on behalf of the unique revelations
which occurred between 1973-1981 with the
sponsorship of the Holy See to the then Cardinal
Ratzinger - now Pope Benedict XVI and received the
word that these apparitions were reliable and worthy
of belief.

The Message - Worldwide Chastisement

Like Fatima, the message of Akita warned of a coming chastisement. But this chastisement, unlike Fatima, was much more biblical in nature. The warnings included apocalypses of biblical proportions. "As I told you, if men do not repent and better themselves, the Father will inflict a terrible punishment on all humanity. It will be a punishment greater than the deluge, such as one will never have seen before. Fire will fall from the sky and will wipe out a great part of humanity, the good as well as the bad, sparing neither priests nor faithful. The survivors will find themselves so desolate that they will envy the dead."

But similar to the apparitions at Garabandal, the manifestation of the Blessed Virgin at Akita, Japan indicated that a sign would be left for all time to prove the presence of God. "The only arms which will remain for you will be the Rosary and the Sign left by my Son. Each day, recite the prayers of the Rosary. With the Rosary, pray for the Pope, the bishops and the priests."

As with many manifestations of the Blessed Virgin Mary, Our Lady of Akita told Sr. Sasagawa that if enough people prayed for peace, and prayed the Rosary in particular, many of these disasters could be averted.

The Manifestation at Akita, Japan

Sr. Agnes Sasagawa began receiving interior locutions when she prayed before a certain statue of the Blessed Virgin in the chapel in the convent at Akita, Japan. This statue began to bleed from a wound in her side and then to cry tears of blood sometime after these interior locutions began taking place.

Our Lady of America
A Humble Nun Received Mystical Knowledge

A special devotion to Mary was propagated through this apparition by the mystic, Sister Mildred Mary Neuzil.

Professed as a religious nun in 1933, Sister Mildred Mary Neuzil engaged in many humble practices before she began to receive the revelations of Our Lady of America.

Her mystical experiences began in 1938 when she began to experience interior locutions, mystical flights and other phenomena. It wasn't until 1948 that these experiences were brought to the attention of her confessor.

The Message of Our Lady of America

Our Lady of America gave messages to Sister Mildred from 1954 to 1981, but unlike other apparitions, the messages cover many subjects: The Indwelling

Trinity, The Sacred Humanity, The Holy Family, Our Lady, St. Joseph, The Angels and Torchbearers of the Queen.

Although she covered many subjects in her apparitions and interior locutions, the actual revelations are contained in a very small diary of only 48 pages containing messages much like this: "Beloved daughter, there is so much untruth in the truth that is sought. Truth comes from Him who has been sent by my Son, the Spirit who is Truth. Pray continuously to be guided by this Spirit who is the true enlightenment." *Our Lady of America*, By Sister Mildred Mary Neuzil

The Blessed Virgin Mary also gave Sister Mildred two prayers; a prayer to the Immaculate Conception and to the Indwelling Most Holy Trinity.

The Manifestations of Our Lady of America

Paintings of Our Lady of America were done by Donna Mae Halsted, a humble woman in Dove Creek, Colorado, USA, who also struck the large statue which was eventually brought to the Basilica of the National Shrine of the Immaculate Conception in Washington, D.C.

Medals have been struck which bear the image of Our Lady of America on one side and a Coat of Arms of the Christian Family on the other. It states "By your

Holy and Immaculate Conception, O Mary, deliver us from evil."

Sister Mildred Mary Neuzil resided in Fostoria, Ohio, USA, where a center has been established to honor her and the apparitions which occurred to her during her life.

Our Lady of Banneux

Apparitions which Immediately Followed Beauraing

Our Lady of Banneux appeared near Belgium and not far from Germany.

The Apparitions at Banneux began almost to the second directly after those at Beauraing came to an end.

In 1933, the Blessed Virgin Mary appeared eight times to Mariette Beco, a twelve year old girl who had ceased going to Catechism classes and had not yet even made her First Holy Communion.

Monsignor Kerkhofs, the bishop of Liege, Belgium where the manifestations took place was quoted as saying "Nevertheless, in the whole village she was the child who seemed to be the farthest from God, and the least prepared for any kind of mystical manifestation."

The Message of Our Lady of Banneux

The Blessed Virgin Mary said "I am the Virgin of the Poor." On other occasions, she gave special graces in the form of steam to Mariette and said that the steam was "for the sick."

As with most apparitions, she gave to Mariette a secret which has never been revealed. Asking her to pray very much, she concluded by telling Mariette to always put her "Faith First."

Our Blessed Lady had asked for a chapel to be built on the location and also said several times, "I come to relieve the suffering." Mariette, being a simple girl, did not at the time understand the word 'relieve,' so she didn't understand until it was stated to her several times.

The Manifestation of Our Lady of Banneux

Our Lady appeared to Mariette in a long white robe with a white coverlet over her head. Golden light surrounded her head and body and a Rosary hung from small blue tie around her waist.

An Episcopal commission investigated the Apparitions of Our Lady of Banneux from 1935 until 1937. A cult was being born which would come to be known as the 'The Cult of the Virgin of the Poor."

The manifestations of Our Lady of Banneux were approved fully by the church in 1949 by Bishop Kerkhofs of Liege and then the Holy See.

Our Lady of Beauraing

The Blessed Virgin Shows Herself Thirty Five Times

Beauraing is near to the French borders, and it was in 1932 that Mary began appearing to five children.

These Apparitions of Our Blessed Lady occurred in Namur, Belgium in 1932 and 1933. In that period of time, the small town boasted about 2400 people. It was at the convent of the sisters of Christian Doctrine of Nancy in a small replica of a Lourdes Grotto that these apparitions occurred.

The Message of Our Lady of Beauraing

The Blessed Virgin Mary told the children to "Always be good." And it was especially important to her that they attend the Mass of the Immaculate Conception for which 15,000 people came. She told them to "Pray, pray very much."

She asked several things of the children including that a chapel be built, she wished for people to come on pilgrimage, she stated "I am the Immaculate Virgin," and she showed them her golden and Immaculate Heart.

During the final days of the apparitions, each child received a secret, none of which have been revealed. But to Fernande Voisin, a fifteen year old visionary, she asked, "Do you love My Son?" To which Fernande replied "Yes." Spectators reported hearing a loud thunderous sound and seeing a ball of fire coming from the sky as this was happening. "Do you love me?" She asked. "Yes," Fernande replied. "Then sacrifice yourself for me."

The Manifestation of Our Lady of Beauraing

Showing herself thirty five times in just a three month period between November 29th of 1932 to January 3 of 1933, she initially came walking upon a viaduct. A few days later she was seen in a rose hawthorn bush by a grille just thirty feet distant from the replica of the Lourdes Grotto.

Five children saw her: Andree Degeimbre, Gilberte Degeimbre, Fernande Voisin, Gilberte Voisin and Albert Voisin. The children ranged in age from eleven to fourteen and one of the unusual aspects of Banneux was the fact that the families of the children were not considered devout although well respected in their community.

She appeared to be about the age of eighteen. Her dress was long, white and pleated with a belt. It reflected some kind of blue light. Her eyes were deep blue and rays of light emanated from her head. On her right arm was a Rosary in all the Apparitions.

Our Lady of Conyers, Georgia

Nancy Fowler was the Messenger in this American Apparition

Nancy Fowler has the unique distinction of receiving detailed messages for years at a time.

Nancy Fowler has the distinction of receiving messages from the Blessed Virgin Mary and Our Lord Jesus Christ. She's received innumerable messages since 1990.

Angel of Peace Prayer from Fatima

One of the strong admonitions Nancy Fowler received from the Blessed Virgin Mary was to "Let this prayer be echoed all over the world." It was a prayer given at the apparitions of Fatima:

"Most Holy Trinity - Father, Son and Holy Spirit - I adore Thee profoundly. I offer Thee the most precious Body, Blood, Soul and Divinity of Jesus Christ, present in all the tabernacles of the world, in reparation for the outrages, sacrileges and indifferences whereby He is offended. And through the infinite merits of His Most Sacred Heart and the Immaculate Heart of Mary, I beg of Thee the conversion of poor sinners."

The Message of Our Lady of Conyers, Georgia

Receiving visions and interior locutions on a monthly basis from the Blessed Virgin Mary and Our Lord Jesus Christ, Nancy Fowlers messages are catalogued on a website: Our Loving Mother. Her messages usually occur on the 13th of the month and many of them contain admonitions to pray, repent and have more faith.

Recent messages from Our Lord Jesus Christ have stated that many new diseases will be coming. And messages from both Our Lord Jesus Christ and the Blessed Virgin Mary have spoken of a great war. They ask the faithful to pray diligently for peace so that the divine justice may be satisfied and that mankind may be spared this tribulation.

The Manifestation of Our Lady of Conyers, Georgia

Nancy Fowler seems to have an unusual gift of experiencing visions, many of them during prayer and the Holy Mass. But she also receives interior locutions, which are clear vocal messages she hears in her spirit.

The monthly messages ceased in October of 1995, but Nancy received a yearly anniversary message through 1998. Her final message on October 13th, 1998 reiterated the words from Portugal, Fatima in 1917. She stated that her requests were the same. In Fatima, the Blessed Mother had asked for the world to pray The Holy Rosary. She had asked that the people pray for peace around the world and the conversion of sinners.

Our Lady of Czestochowa

St. Luke the Evangelist is Believed to have Painted
this Image

Legend states that Mary told St. Luke about the life of
Jesus while he painted her.

The next mention of Our Lady of Czestochowa occurs
in 326 A.D. when St. Helen found it in Jerusalem and
gave it to her son, having a shrine built in
Constantinople to house it.

The Unusual Lineage of Our Lady of Czestochowa

Legend tells us, that the original and first Black
Madonna to be made into an icon came after St. Luke
the Evangelist experienced an apparition of the
Blessed Virgin Mary and painted her. While painting

the image, it is said that the Holy Virgin related to St. Luke the life of Jesus which he later incorporated into the Gospel of St. Luke in the New Testament.

The original image is kept safe for public viewing at the Marian Shrine in Poland and many miracles are attributed to it which have been well documented since 1382.

Ladislaus of Opole is credited with bringing the sacred and famous image to Poland in the year 1382 and attaining the sacred protection of the Monks of St. Paul the First Hermit from Hungary. Currently, the shrine is maintained by the Pauline Fathers and Brothers.

The Message of Our Lady of Czestochowa

The Blessed Virgin has spoken through this most holy Polish relic in a different way than in some of the other apparition stories. Her original intent was to help St. Luke in recording the Gospel of the Lord Jesus Christ.

But the image of Our Lady of Czestochowa has withstood many attempts to have it destroyed. Wars, pillaging marauders and other evildoers have made many attempts throughout the centuries to destroy the image and the monastery which enshrines it. But on every occasion the image was preserved.

A famous attack in the year 1430 A.D. left two slashes in the face of the beautiful Black Madonna, and despite the attempts of art historians to repair these marks, they have remained perhaps as a sign of the Blessed Virgin's resilience in the face of such attempts to destroy the message she came to deliver and subsequently represent for centuries to come in an image which has not only survived but thrived for just under 2,000 years.

After World War II, the Polish people derived much strength from Our Lady of Czestochowa to rebuild their lives and their country.

Our Lady of Fatima

The Three Young Visionaries of 1917

It was while watching their sheep that three young children, Francesco, Jacinta and Lucia experienced a Marian Apparition.

Three shepherd children in the tiny village of Fatima, Portugal received a series of six apparitions of the Blessed Virgin Mary, St. Joseph, St. Michael the Archangel and a beautiful Angel of the Eucharist for six consecutive months on the 13th day, beginning in May 1917.

The Message of Our Lady of Fatima

Our Lady of Fatima appeared with a Rosary around her waist and asked the children to tell people to pray the daily family rosary for peace. She also asked the children for the consecration of Russia to her Immaculate Heart, which was finally accomplished July 17th, 1952 by Pope Pius XII.

Pope John Paul II had a special veneration for Our Lady of Fatima, as the day of the attempt made upon his life occurred on the anniversary of these apparitions and he felt that Our Lady of Fatima had saved his life. He made a special pilgrimage to Fatima after his recovery to thank her.

As a result of his unique devotion to Our Lady of Fatima, Pope John Paul II made profound efforts to bring down the iron curtain in Russia and is credited with being the man behind the fall of communism in the former Soviet Union.

The Secrets of Our Lady of Fatima

Three secrets were revealed at Fatima, the first two were revealed immediately, while the third was to remain sealed until 1960's when Sister Lucia – the only one of the child visionaries to live into adulthood – said the Pope would have permission to reveal it. But it was not immediately revealed and much controversy surrounded the contents of that secret.

The first two secrets consisted of a vision of hell and the means by which souls can be saved from hell.

Regarding the first secret, the children related "Our Lady showed us a great sea of fire which seemed to be under the earth. Plunged into this fire were demons and souls in human form, like transparent burning embers, all blackened or burnished bronze, floating about in the conflagration . . . "

The Blessed Virgin Mary asked for a devotion to be established to her Immaculate Heart and a Communion of Reparation on the First Saturdays of every month to save sinners from this fate. She asked again for the Daily Family Rosary to be recited as it would save many souls.

The Manifestation of Our Lady of Fatima and the Miracle of the Sun

Our Lady of Fatima appeared to the shepherd children in a white robe adorning her body and head, with a blue tassel around her waist holding a Rosary. In subsequent visions, the children were given visions of St. Joseph, St. Michael the Archangel and a unique angel who they termed the Angel of the Eucharist who presented them with Holy Communion.

On the day of the last apparition, the Miracle of the Sun occurred. Although it had been pouring rain all day, 70,000 people bore witness to the sun dancing in the sky, turning radiant colors and coming to earth as if they were to collide and then immediately pulling back into the heavens. When it was over, the ground and everybody present were completely dry.

Our Lady of Garabandal
Four Young Girls became Visionaries in 1961, Spain

In the writings left behind about the apparitions, the visionaries said that the messages they received were about prayer, penance and Eucharist.

Four girls in the town of San Sebastian, Garabandal, Spain – a town of only 300 people – first saw the Blessed Virgin on June 18, 1961.

Who were the Visionaries?

All the girls were unrelated despite some similar names, around the ages of eleven and twelve and all from profoundly poor families: Conchita Gonzalez, Maria Dolores Mazon, Jacinta Gonzalez and Maria Cruz Gonzalez.

The Manifestations of Our Lady of Garabandal

Playing on the outskirts of town, the girls heard a sudden loud sound, like that of thunder. Before they could discern what was happening, the Archangel

Michael appeared to them in a luminous form. The following day, the Archangel Michael appeared to them again and told them they would meet the Blessed Virgin Mary on July 2nd, 1961.

Because so many had heard of the upcoming apparition, many had come to witness the event. Even cameras caught the event on film, and you can see many miraculous manifestations in these films. For instance, the girls all fell into an ecstasy and when the girls receive the Holy Communion from St. Michael the Archangel, you can see a host miraculous appear on their tongues as they receive it.

The girls described what they had seen thus:

"She is dressed in a white robe with a blue mantle and a crown of golden stars. Her hands are slender. There is a brown scapular on her right arm, except when she carried the Child Jesus in her arms. Her hair, deep nut-brown, is parted in the center. Her face is long, with a fine nose. Her mouth is very pretty with lips a bit thin. She looks like a girl of eighteen. She is rather tall. There is no voice like hers. No woman is just like her, either in the voice or the face or anything else. Our Lady Manifested herself as Our Lady of Carmel."

The Message of Our Lady of Garabandal

The warnings our Blessed Virgin had for the girls at Garabandal were frightening to say the least. They spoke of a chastisement to come upon all mankind, but before this something of a graver nature. A sign would appear in the sky, the visionaries said, which would somehow reveal to every human being their own sinfulness. Conchita wrote about this miracle, "It will be a "correction" of our conscience. It will cause great fear and will make us reflect within ourselves on the consequences of our own personal sins."

The Blessed Lady was disappointed in the little attention given to her words of warning at Garabandal, and in her final messages rebuked Catholics and Priests who did not properly honor the Holy Eucharist.

The girls were given a vision of great horror where they saw the potential chastisements to come upon the world if people did not begin to pray, fast and do penance for their sins and the sins of the world.

Our Lady of Good Counsel

The Mother of Tenderness

The story of Our Lady of Good Counsel begins in Genazzano, Italy in 1467.

Between 1621 and 1629, a chapel was built to hold the honored image of Our Lady of Good Counsel next to the Church in Genazzano, Italy where it had been previously kept.

The Manifestation of Our Lady of Good Counsel

Another title for the image of Our Lady of Good Counsel is the word 'Eleousa' which means the Mother of Tenderness. In the image, Mary and the Baby Jesus nestle close to one another in a manner which is often referred to as showing the intimacy of breastfeeding.

There are two stories around Our Lady of Good Counsel, and it is not known which story carries the higher strand of truth.

The story begins in Albania where Our Lady of Good Counsel was venerated as Our Lady of Shkodra. The ancient icon inspired such love of the Blessed Mother, that many were drawn to it as a devotional work which inspired the intense feelings of the love of the Mother of God to all her children.

Many people prayed before the image, oftentimes asking for protection for armies fighting invading forces from other countries.

A miraculous occurrence happened one day when two soldiers came in to pray before the Blessed Lady's image which they reported to miraculous move away from the wall. They followed the image as it travelled all the way to Genazzano, where they chose to settle away from the invading Turks who overcame their home country.

But a second strand to the stories begins here. Petruccia de Geneo, a local widow in Genazanno found herself called to help repair the church where the image had been kept which had fallen into disrepair. But her money was all spent before the building was finished, leaving an entire wall undone.

On April 25, 1467, the Feast Day of St. Mark, the city was participating in a yearly festival when a fantastic miracle occurred at the Church of Our Lady of Good Counsel. At 4:00, they saw a mysterious cloud come down from heaven completely encompassing the unfinished wall of the church. When they dissipated, the image of Our Lady of Good Counsel was standing tall above the unfinished wall and the city bells rang without the aid of human hands.

The Message of Our Lady of Good Counsel

The most common prayer to Our Lady of Good Counsel is "Mother of Good Counsel, return to us. On the path of peace, lead us." Many devotions to Our Lady of Good Counsel have evolved over the years. "O Mary of Good Counsel, inflame the hearts of all who are devoted to you, so that all of them have shelter in you, O great Mother of God. O most worthy Lady, let everyone choose you as teacher and wise counselor of their souls, since you are, as Saint Augustine says, the counsel of the Apostles and counsel of all peoples. Amen."

Perhaps the most striking sign of the impact of Our Lady of Good Counsel is the fact that prayers to her are included in some of the liturgies of the Catholic Church.

Our Lady of Guadalupe
Mother of the Americas

Our Lady of Guadalupe was meant to bring the Indian people of South and Central America to the Catholic faith.

The apparition of Our Lady of Guadalupe is unique in Church history. The Blessed Virgin Mary appeared to a humble peasant Indian man on Tepeyac hill in Mexico two times from December 9th to December 12th 1531 A.D.

The Manifestation of Our Lady of Guadalupe

Blessed Juan Diego was crossing the hill of Tepeyac to return home from Mexico City. During his walk, he noticed something very unusual. A young woman about the age of sixteen appeared all surrounded in light appeared at the top of the hill. Because it was winter, the landscape was fairly barren and this image definitely caught his attention.

When he approached her, she asked that a chapel be built on the very spot in honor of her. It was at this moment that he realized this was the Blessed Virgin Mary. She came looking pregnant, wearing an inner garment of an orangish – pink with many spectacular designs upon it. Her outer garment was turquoise – green with stars scattered all about it and gilded in gold. Surrounding her were the rays of the sun. Her face was dark like the Native Indians of Mexico.

The Blessed Virgin sent Juan Diego to speak to the local Bishop about her requests. And when he arrived, the Bishop gave him little notice except to ask that the Blessed Virgin give him a miraculous sign.

The following day, he again came across the very same Tepeyac hill to find the Blessed Virgin waiting for him again. When asked to produce a miracle, she immediately was able to make all the roses bloom in the midst of winter – many beautifully colored roses. Juan Diego gathered these miraculous roses into his tilma, the garment he wore in hopes of bringing them to the Bishop.

When he arrived at the Church, he planned to open his tilma and allow the miraculous roses to fall to the floor. Ironically, when he did so, the bishop recognized them as Castilian roses, which were not native to the area, but were native to where he had grown up. But no roses ever grew at this time of year on Tepeyac Hill, and there was something much more astonishing for them to see.

Emblazoned upon the tilma of Juan Diego was the image of the Blessed Virgin Mary in living color. That same garment remains intact today, even though it was made of a cloth which normally decomposes within 30 – 40 years. It is enshrined in the Cathedral of Our Lady of Guadalupe and remains a testament to God's creative genius.

The Message of Our Lady of Guadalupe

Many of the Aztec Indians had lost their beliefs after the Spanish conquest of their peoples. It was Our Lady of Guadalupe, appearing through the humble Indian man – who gave an open invitation to all the native peoples that they were her children, too. Our Lady of Guadalupe is loved and revered the world over, but especially in Mexico, and Central and South America. Our Lady of Guadalupe brought the people together and gave them a home in the Catholic Faith.

Our Lady of Hungary
An Astonishing Apparition Caught on Film

Our Lady of Hungary was captured on film by a builder and his photographer who were planning to restore an old church.

What is fascinating about Our Lady of Hungary is that it is one of the few and very rare photographs that have been taken which actually completely convey the presence of the Blessed Virgin Mary within them. There is nothing subtle about this apparition.

The Manifestation of Our Lady of Hungary

On September 3, 1989, a team of church restorers were sent in to work on a beautiful cathedral. They were bringing in ladders, photographers, construction workers, along with the actual restoration specialist to take a look and see how much work would be required and necessary to bring this church back up to par.

When the restorer and the photographer were alone in the building by the altar, the restoration expert began walking across the altar looking around at what might be necessary to complete this project when he suddenly noticed something. Shouting to the photographer, he said, "Do you see that!" The photographer could see nothing, but the restorer wasted no time in shouting, "Take a picture of me right here. Take a picture of me right here." He did and the rest became history.

One of the most spectacular apparition photographs appeared; a clear image of the Blessed Virgin Mary – all in light – her head surrounded with a crown of twelve stars. Her light radiated across much of the altar.

The team was stunned and the apparition became quickly known as Our Lady of Hungary.

The Message of Our Lady of Hungary

Because Our Lady of Hungary never spoke, her message clearly became a powerful silence. She'd appeared in perfect order with the Revelation of St. John and the image was something unlike any of them had ever seen. As it began to be passed around the world, it soon became a phenomenon everywhere because of its clear and obvious quality, the undeniable miraculous nature of this photograph.

Our Lady of La Salette

Supernatural Manifestations in the Alpine Section of Dauphine

On September 19, 1846, Our Blessed Mother came to speak to two children who had been hired as cowherds.

In a small town of 300 inhabitants by the name of La Salette – Fallavaux (Isere France), the Blessed Virgin came to speak to Maximim Giraud, an eleven year old child, and Melanie Calvat, who was fifteen. They didn't know each other well and had actually only been acquainted for a few days when the apparitions began.

The Manifestation of Our Lady of La Salette

While watching animals on the mountainside as cowherds, around 3:30 PM a beautiful lady appeared to them. She would appear on what they called 'paradises,' which were heaps of stones in the form of altars covered in flowers. She pointed them in the direction of a place called 'The Little Fountain' which they hurriedly rushed off to.

Immediately, they saw a beautiful and radiant globe of light which opened up and afterwards a woman sitting on the stones. Her hair was pulled back by a diadem and a wreath of roses. A white kerchief also covered in roses lay on her head and covered her shoulders.

She wore a gleaming white dress which seemed to emanate the essence of gold. A crucifix was adorned around her neck and she seemed to also wear a chain which bore great weight upon her shoulders.

The Message of Our Lady of La Salette

The message received by the children at La Salette was lengthy. It was a message of chastisements to come if sinners did not convert. But the Blessed Virgin was very specific.

"If my people do not willingly submit, I shall be forced to allow the arm of my Son to weight down! For how long a time have I been grieved because of you. I have had to pray unceasingly lest my Son abandon you. You can never understand how much sorrow I have known." She said. Because of the profundity of her message, Our Lady of La Salette is known as the 'Weeping Virgin.'

In her admonitions, she spoke of simple things like the failure to observe God on Sundays, and people swearing left and right with impatience and ingratitude. She spoke also of gluttony and how much it disgusted the divine majesty, referring to men who "devour meat like dogs." She said that crops would fail no matter what if souls were to continue down the path they were following but that "If sinners will be converted, the very stone and rocks will be changed into heaps of grain, and the potato fields will be rich and will bear abundantly."

She admonished the children to pray every morning and to go to Mass whenever possible. And finally, she sent private messages to the Pope of which we know very little except that it appeared to be a profound correction of the Papacy and ecclesiastics in their contradictory ways of life.

Pope Pius IX read the note and was noted to acknowledge fault in all that was pointed out to him about his own failings and that of the Church. He always approved the happenings at La Salette.

Although the contents of those messages were never put into public circulation, they were allowed to be published for the purpose of priests. Pope Pius IX felt that it could do all priests much good to read them.

Our Lady of Lourdes
A Humble Girl who Discovered a Healing Spring

Bernadette Soubirous was the most unlikely candidate for a Marian apparition.

But it happened anyway on February 11, 1858 to a young girl sickly from birth with bad asthma who never studied her catechism.

The location of the apparitions has become one of the most visited apparition sites around the world due primarily to the healing properties of the spring water which was discovered there during the eighteen visits the Blessed Virgin Mary made to the humble and poor girl.

The Manifestation of Our Lady of Lourdes

The eighteen apparitions occurred between February 11, 1858 to July 16th, 1858. It first occurred as she was off gathering wood for the family fire and was led to a grotto, the hollow rock of Massabielle. St. Bernadette described her as a lady "lovelier than I have ever seen." She was wearing all white, with a blue sash tied around her waist carrying a rosary on her right arm.

The Lady told Bernadette to drink from the water of a fountain within the grotto which was as yet unknown. Bernadette began scratching on the ground in a fury, and although much time passed, suddenly a spring emerged from the ground. Within a short time, it was gushing with water and people began to come on pilgrimage from around the world to bring their sick and dying in hopes of a potential cure.

The Message of Our Lady of Lourdes

Perhaps one of the most important messages besides that of the Blessed Lady's desire to heal the sick and suffering and to bring spiritual comfort to all mankind, was a secret that she revealed to St. Bernadette. Because Bernadette was so uncatechized and simple, the selection of her to receive the message was absolutely a manifestation of God's Mysterious Ways.

At the time, the Pope was considering adding a dogma to church teaching about the Immaculate Conception of the Blessed Virgin Mary, claiming that she, too, was born without sin. But he was unsure if this was God's will, and was waiting for a sign.

One day, the Blessed Lady told Bernadette to tell the priest who knew of these theological debates and discussions going on in the papacy to tell them "The Immaculate Conception has sent you." The priest immediately understood the importance of these words, and the message was spread to the Pope who took it as his sign to approve of the dogma which has been in place ever since.

Another fascinating aspect of St. Bernadette and her apparitions is that she became an incorruptible after her death. Many still go to the shrine of Lourdes to receive of the healing waters, but just as many go to witness her perfectly incorrupt body preserved in a shrine.

Our Lady of Medjugorje

An Apparition that Never Stops Giving

It began in the middle of the 1980's when eight young children began to hear the voices of Mary and have not ceased since.

Medjugorje is credited with creating more priestly and religious vocations in the Church since the early 1990's than anyone or anything else.

The Manifestation of Our Lady of Medjugorje

The visions began in the early evening of June 24, 1981 on what is now famously known as Podbrdo hill. People come from all over the world to climb the hill where the first and many of the successive apparitions took place. Crosses, rosaries and other Catholic sacramentals are strewn all over the steep and rocky pathway to the peak.

The list of the visionaries and their year of birth is as follows: Vicka Ivankovic – 1964; Mirjana Dragicevic – 1965; Marija Pavlovic – 1965; Ivanka Ivankovic – 1966; Ivan Dragicevic – 1965; Jakov Colo – 1971. Two other visionaries who do not visually see the Blessed Virgin Mary, but hear her voice interiorly are Jelena Vasilj – 10972 and Marijana Vasilj – 1972.

Our Lady of Medjugorje appeared to the first six of the eight visionaries on that day in 1981 as a "white figure immersed in a glowing, golden and shining cloud. She announced herself as the 'Queen of Peace.'

Although the communist regime of the time tried very hard to suppress the mystics and the visions themselves, they were unable to quelch the growing interest in continuing messages from the Blessed Mother.

Our Lady of Medjugorje told the visionaries about the Croatian wars which were to come years before they happened.

The visionaries at Medjugorje have an exceptional parish priest – considered the most famous living parish priest in the world – who has supported and helped them from the very beginning even going to jail and forced labor camps rather than denounce the message of the Blessed Virgin Mary given to the visionaries – Father Jozo Zovko.

The Message of Our Lady of Medjugorje

Our Lady of Medjugorje spoke about the catastrophes to come, not only in the Croatian regions but around the world, and explained that the lack of faith in God was directly responsible for these coming difficult times. She prescribed a very strict code of penance, prayer, fasting, reparation and engaging in the sacraments frequently – including monthly confession – as a way to begin to change our society which was fast losing its faith and respect of God.

Our Lady of Medjugorje still speaks today, although only a few of the visionaries still receive regular apparitions. People from around the world continue to flock to Medjugorje to be present during the daily messages and to receive the special graces that are received from being present in such a holy place.

Our Lady of Mount Carmel

A Devotion Instituted by the Carmelites

In honor of the official recognition finally given to their order, the Carmelites instituted the Feast day of Our Lady of Mount Carmel.

Saint Simon Stock received Our Lady of Mount Carmel after praying fervently for his struggling order in the year 1251.

The Manifestation of Our Lady of Mount Carmel

Our Lady of Mount Carmel is profoundly identifiable with her deep brown interior robe and an exterior blue or white garment, depending on the artist who paints her. Upon her head is placed a tall, shining and golden crown. The baby Jesus is in her left hand and both of them are surrounded in profound light. Many of the images of Our Lady of Mount Carmel also appear with the crown of twelve stars around the high heavenly crown.

Our Blessed Lady appeared to Simon Stock carrying what has commonly become known to the world today as a Scapular, but this saint was the first to receive it. It has two square pieces one on each end of a middle double string.

One of the squares contains an image of St. Simon Stock bowing before Our Lady of Mount Carmel and says "Behold the Sign of Salvation, Our Lady of Mount Carmel."

The other square states "Behold the sign of Salvation: Put on the Lord Jesus Christ."

It is believed that scapulars originated with the Benedictine Order which began as a simple piece of cloth representing consecration to the Lord but then evolved into many kinds of religious garments and habits.

But the Scapular of Our Lady of Mount Carmel is by far the most widely known and worn around the world by Catholics for its special promises given by the Blessed Lady.

The Message of Our Lady of Mount Carmel

Our Blessed Lady instructed St. Simon Stock that those who would wear her scapular and pray certain prayers would never suffer eternal fire, i.e. hell. They would be protected especially by the Blessed Virgin Mary at the moment of their death.

Handing St. Simon Stock the scapular, her exact words were these: "Take, beloved son, this scapular of thine order as a badge of my confraternity and for thee and all Carmelites a special sign of grace; whoever dies in this garment will not suffer everlasting fire, it is the sign of salvation, a safeguard in dangers, a pledge of peace and of the covenant."

Our Lady of Pellevoisin

The Queen of Heaven appears to a Country Village

Estelle Faguette began to see apparitions of Mary while dying of consumption.

In the Diocese of Bourges, France in 1876, a maid who was in the depths of the dying process from a horrible disease of the time known as consumption, had a miraculous recovery and lived another fifty years.

The Manifestation of Our Lady of Pellevoisin

Estelle experienced a total of fifteen visions in the same year. Our Blessed Lady appeared in a mantle all white with what appear to be white rose petals showering from both of her hands in front of her.

The Message of Our Lady of Pellevoisin

"If you want to serve me, be simple, and let your words and deeds agree", Estelle reported that the Blessed Virgin Mary told her. She also expressed grave concern about the neglect of the people towards her Son in the Blessed Sacrament and all forms of prayer.

A white scapular came to be associated with this apparition containing the image of Our Lady of Pellevoisin on one side wearing the garb of all white with the white rose petals coming from her hands, and on the other side, an image of the Sacred Heart of Jesus. Estelle said the Blessed Lady asked her to tell others to wear it in reparation to Our Lord Jesus Christ.

Years later, the confraternity of Mary, Mother of Mercy, approved and instituted the use but Pellevoisin and the apparitions there were kept out of their decree. It was disallowed that any statues or images of Our Lady of Pellevoisin be made with her wearing this scapular.

No official report has ever been made by the archbishops of Bourges about these visions or Estelle Faguette's visions. Vatican authorities have remained quiet, as well.

Despite this, pilgrims still come to the commemorative chapel at Pellevoisin. There are three known churches which honor Our Lady of Pellevoisin; a shrine of Our Lady of Pellevoisin in New York City, a chapel in St. Paul's church, New York City; and there is a church by the name of Our Lady of Pellevoisin in McIntosh, Ontario, Canada.

Our Lady of Pontmain
The Lady with the Stars in the Sky

Our Lady of Pontmain is a unique apparition of Mary who is reported to never take her face off the Cross of Christ.

It was during the Franco Prussian War in January 1871 that the Apparitions of Our Lady of Pontmain began. Beginning under less than ample circumstances, the people of the small town of about five hundred people were very saddened that so many of their young men had been called off to war and 2/3 of the country was under the control of the German Army.

The Manifestation of Our Lady of Pontmain

Four children witnessed the apparition to come, Joseph Barbedette, Eugene Barbedette, Francoise Richer and Jeanne-Marie Lebrosse. Joseph described the apparition as follows: "In the air, seven or eight metres above Augustin Guidecoq's house, I saw a woman of extraordinary beauty."

He went on to describe her as young, tall and clad in a garment of deep blue. Her dress was covered with pentagonal shaped gold stars of great brilliance, and her head was adorned with a black veil. Above her head was a golden crown which described as "resembling a diadem."

All the children described her as having profoundly deep and loving eyes, her face adorned with "smiles of sweetness." Joseph had said "Like a true mother, she seemed happier in looking at us than we in contemplating her."

The Message of Our Lady of Pontmain

At Pontmain, the message received was primarily non-verbal and can only be surmised by taking a close interpretation of her actions. The only words spoken by the Blessed Lady were these: "Pray, my children." At the time of the apparition, a congregation of local inhabitants had been singing a hymn. When they arrived at the words "My Sweet Jesus, now has come the time to grant thy pardon to our heavy hearts," the Blessed Virgin was said to have a "shadow of sadness" fall upon her face and across her entire personage.

Holding up a red cross before her chest, the image of Jesus Christ was upon it with His name in red lettering. She said nothing but appeared to be praying as her lips were moving.

Our Lady of Pontmain was declared a valid apparition by the Bishop and the Holy See and permitted liturgical honors to be given in their diocese under the title of 'Our Lady of Hope of Pontmain.' Plans were also made to erect a shrine in the Blessed Virgin's honor.

Our Lady of Reconciliation
Appeared to a Stigmatist in Betania, Venezuela

Mystic, Maria Esperanza Biancini is the visionary who drew thousands to witness Mary's appearances in Venezuela.

Our Lady of Reconciliation was a very unique apparition in that she appeared as "Our Lady of Lourdes," "Our Lady of Mt. Carmel," "Our Lady of Sorrows," or as "Our Lady of Grace" on different occasions.

"Our Lady, Reconciler of People and of Nations" is another name given to this modern apparition in Betania where pilgrims still flock to see the Blessed Virgin Mary and hear her messages.

The Manifestation of Our Lady of Reconciliation

Although the visionary, Maria Esperanza Biancini passed away in 2004 after a long bout with illness, people still flock to the special site in Betania,

Venezuela where the Apparitions of the Blessed Virgin Mary have been occurring since well before 1987 when they were approved by the Catholic Church.

The Blessed Virgin manifested herself to Maria Esperanza Biancini as 'Mary, Virgin and mother, Reconciler of all Peoples and Nations.' Because she came to Maria in so many forms – appearing as she had in previous apparitions – her image as Our Lady of Reconciliation remains a bit undefined.

Many miracles occurred during the life of the mystic including an unusual phenomenon where roses spontaneously burst from her heart. This is reported to have occurred in the presence of witnesses sixteen times. The Eucharistic Host was known to miraculously materialize upon her tongue and many people reported the scent of roses around the visionary many times.

The Message of Our Lady of Reconciliation

Since Maria Esperanza received so many messages, often on a daily basis for over 20 years, it is difficult to summarize them. But the primary urgings of the Blessed Virgin Mary to those who came to listen to her included exhorting the faithful to engage in frequent sacraments, go to confession regularly and try to be more understanding of other people around the world.

Included in the apparitions were many prophecies of wars and historic events which did come to pass.

Our Lady of Soufanieh

Mary appears in the City of St. Paul's conversion,
Damascus, Syria

Myrna Nazour has been having visions of the Blessed
Virgin. She now bears the Stigmata and her icon cries
tears of oil.

Five initial apparitions of the Holy Blessed Virgin
Mary occurred to Myrna Nazour only four of which
contained actual messages. But she continued to
receive messages up until April 10, 2004.

The Manifestation of Our Lady of Soufanieh

In the Apparitions of Our Lady of Soufanieh, a globe
of light was the first thing to appear to the visionary.
The Blessed Virgin herself manifested upon the
branch of a eucalyptus tree, but only after a blue

crescent appeared before her. Sitting on the branch of the tree, the Virgin Mary then stood and walked towards the terrace of the home and crossed an iron railing before stopping to speak.

Her dress was white with a blue belt and she wore a hood which formed part of her dress over her shoulder along with a blue shawl. In her right hand, she held a crystal rosary. Her right arm was folded at her chest and her left arm hung down to the side, her feet remaining out of view.

The Message of Our Lady of Soufanieh

The Blessed Virgin Mary appeared five times on December 15th and 18th 1982 and January 8th, February 21st and March 24th 1983. Since the messages ceased, the holy icons continued to spill out holy oil and the visionary, Myrna Nazour, was struck with the marks of Jesus Christ – the Holy Stigmata.

Among the many message of peace and continual prayer, The Blessed Virgin Mary gave Myrna a special prayer for the faithful to pray:

> *"Beloved Jesus,*
> *Grant that I rest in You above all things,*
> *above all creatures,*
> *above all Your angels,*
> *above all praise,*
> *above all rejoicing and exultation,*
> *above all glory and honour,*
> *above all heavenly hosts,*

For You alone are the Most High,
You alone are the Almighty and Good above
all things.
May You come to me and relieve me,
and release me from my chains,
and grant me freedom,
because without You my joy is not complete,
without You my table is empty."

Our Lady of the Americas

An American Shrine to the Mother of God

Estela Ruiz of Phoenix, Arizona began seeing the Blessed Virgin Mary on December 3rd, 1988.

While visiting Medjugorje in 1988, Estela Ruiz heard the voice of the Blessed Virgin Mary for the first time apparently through a portrait of Our Lady of Guadalupe. It said to her, "Good morning, daughter."

Estela was an unlikely candidate for such apparitions because she was skeptical of all such things and had only gone to Medjugorje under duress from her husband. In fact, she was concerned that her husband was becoming too fanatical about his faith.

Estela was a former school administrator, holding a Masters Degree in Education and her husband had opened a school for poor children. When the apparitions came upon them, it was the last thing this couple with seven children were expecting.

The Manifestation of Our Lady of the Americas

Estela describes the Blessed Virgin thusly: "Her face is slightly round, very beautiful and radiates affection and concern, while her voice is soft and uplifting, with a gentle maternal tone . . . while Mary appears small and delicate, she actually comes across as a strong and powerful woman. Despite her strength, though, the Virgin radiates a femininity that is total. She is kind and humble, yet strong and confident."

According to Estela, the Blessed Virgin Mary appeared to her with long brown hair covered by a veil. Her entire presence was bathed in "streams of brilliant light." Estela Ruiz often said that Our Lady was so brilliant that when she would come and appear to her, it was very much like the dawn of the sun.

The Message of Our Lady of the Americas

The apparitions of Our Lady of the Americas have not yet been approved by the church due to lack of enough hard evidence regarding their supernatural nature. But the local bishop has allowed that the messages be distributed.

Many of the messages pertain to the United States and the moral corruption therein. Warnings were given over the years regarding the wars and natural disasters which have overcome the world. Mary repeatedly told Estela that the world would be devastated by man, not by God – man's "hatred, anger and lack of respect for one another and our beliefs and faiths" would be its downfall, not God's wrath.

The majority of the messages that Estela Ruiz received have been profound witnesses to the need of those in America to turn back to God.

Our Lady of the Miraculous Medal

Catherine Laboure receives the Blessed Virgin in the Chapel

It was the last thing the simple nun, Catherine, expected when a young girl appeared in her cell to lead her to the convent chapel.

In fact, it wasn't until after her death that it was made known that she was the mystic of the Miraculous Medal.

The Manifestation of Our Lady of the Miraculous Medal

The story of the Miraculous Medal is unique and interesting. On the night of July 18 and 19th, 1830, the now Canonized Catherine Laboure was woken up in the middle of the night in the convent of the Daughters of Charity in Paris. The little girl, whom many have discerned may have been a guardian angel of Catherine's, led Catherine silently in the night to the chapel where the Blessed Virgin Mary appeared as the Lady of Grace.

Upon her head was a blue veil, a white undergarment below it. Her hands were outstretched towards the world. On her fingers were many beautiful rings. Some of the rings shone with splendid glory, while others were quite dim. When Catherine asked the meaning of this, the Blessed Lady told her that the rings represented the graces which humankind could ask of her. Those well lit were graces asked for often, while those which were dim were graces people forgot to ask for.

In this first apparition of what would be many, the Blessed Virgin Mary entrusted Catherine with an important mission, the devotion to the Miraculous Medal.

The Message of Our Lady of the Miraculous Medal

Catherine Laboure saw the image of Mary standing on the world and crushing the serpent beneath her feet. Another image showed the cross underscored by a bar and an 'M' for Mary. The Sacred and Immaculate hearts of Jesus and Mary are below. On the front of the medal contains the message: "O Mary, conceived without sin, pray for us who have recourse to thee."

The Blessed Virgin told Catherine to "Have a medal struck upon this model. Those who wear it will receive great graces, especially if they wear it around their neck."

After the medal was distributed, so many miracles of conversion and healing occurred that it became known as 'The Miraculous Medal."

Our Lady of the Pillar
A Vision of St. James

Having trouble with his mission, St. James saw the Blessed Lady upon a pillar carried by angels accompanying him to Jerusalem.

The Apostles of Christ began spreading the gospel message all around the known world shortly after the crucifixion, resurrection and then ascension of their Lord and Master, Jesus Christ. They spread the message throughout Israel and then conquered the entire Roman Empire.

In the village of Saragossa in the Northeastern region of Spain, James, the apostle had traveled far to bring the message of the gospel to the farthest corners of the world. Having been on such a long journey, the Apostle James became dispirited because he felt that his mission had been a failure.

The Manifestation of Our Lady of the Pillar

While in deep prayer, St. James was lamenting what he perceived as failure when the Blessed Holy Virgin appeared to him. She handed him a small wooden statue of herself along with an inexplicable column of wooden jasper.

The Message of Our Lady of the Pillar

Instructing St. James to built a church, the Blessed Virgin Mary said: "This place is to be my house, and this image and column shall be the title and altar of the temple that you shall build."

On special occasions, the wooden statue and jasper column are brought out for public viewing. Our Lady of the Pillar's chapel was the first Church to be dedicated in honor of the Blessed Virgin Mary. It was built about a year after the apparition when St. James sought out to fulfill her wishes.

St. James was the first of the twelve apostles to be martyred for preaching the gospel. It occurred in 44 A.D. by Herod Agrippa after he returned to his home of Jerusalem. St. James was buried in a field, and was not rediscovered until a holy hermit eight centuries later noticed an unusual star formation over a portion of that same field. When they discovered the grave of St. James, they built the Compostella Cathedral on the spot. 'Compostella' meant 'starry field.'

Our Lady of the Rosary

Mary Reveales a Devotion to a Saint

The origin of this name for Mary goes back to an apparition of the Blessed Virgin to St. Dominic in 1208 in the city of Prouille.

Also known as Our Lady of Victory, Our Lady of the Rosary originated from a vision given to St. Dominic in Prouille, France in the year 1208 A.D.

The Manifestation of Our Lady of the Rosary

Our Lady of the Rosary appears in an atypical and beautiful display of her profound power, usually in robes of blue and white. Surrounding her image, are the mysteries of the Rosary as recited in 'The Holy Rosary.' There are a total of fifteen mysteries in the

Rosary and they are depicted in lifelike circular images around her total essence. She is often also wearing a crown – sometimes with twelve stars.

The fifteen mysteries depicted around Our Lady of the Rosary are: (Joyful) The Annunciation, The Visitation, The Nativity, The Presentation, Finding in the Temple, (Sorrowful) Agony in the Garden, Scourging at the Pillar, Crowning with Thorns, Carrying of the Cross, The Crucifixion, (Glorious) The Resurrection, The Ascension, The Descent of the Holy Spirit, The Assumption, the Coronation of the Blessed Virgin Mary, (Luminous) The Baptism of Jesus, The Wedding at Cana, Proclamation of the Kingdom, The Transfiguration, Institution of the Eucharist.

The Message of Our Lady of the Rosary

St. Dominic had retreated into the forest to pray for the conversion of the Albigensians, a heretical sect in the Catholic Church, when a vision of Our Lady appeared to him. She was accompanied by angels and the Blessed Virgin said to him: "Dear Dominic, do you know which weapon the Blessed Trinity wants to use to reform the world." Saint Dominic replied that he could not possibly know such a thing and only she could enlighten him as to the matter.

"I want you to know that, in this kind of warfare, the battering ram has been the Angelic Psalter which is the foundation stone of the New Testament. Therefore if you want to reach these hardened souls and win them over to God, preach my Psalter. "

Arising from the ground and ready to go, invisible angels gathered the people from around the countryside to listen to St. Dominic preach. Many miracles and wonders occurred during this sermon.

Our Lady of the Roses

The Seer of Bayside, New York

Veronica Leuken who lived from 1923 to 1995 was a wife and mother of five in addition to being the messenger of Mary.

Known as the seer of Bayside, Veronica Leuken began having unusual experiences in 1968 when St. Therese, 'The Little Flower,' appeared to her and told her to write down her poems and the things she would see. Leuken was a wife and mother of five children in Bayside, New York, USA.

The Manifestation of Our Lady of the Roses

In the first vision of Our Blessed Lady, the Virgin Mary asked Veronica Leuken to hold prayer vigils at a local church which began in 1970 and continue today, at the St. Robert Bellarmine Church and to have special "Rosary Vigils on the Eve of Feast Days."

These were to commence for the purpose of prayer, penance and atonement.

Our Lady of the Roses appeared to Veronica Leuken as Our Lady of Grace with a wreath of roses around her forehead. On the statues depicted of Our Lady of the Roses, Mary has fresh flower wreaths placed around her head regularly.

The Message of Our Lady of the Roses

Veronica Leuken was told by the Blessed Virgin Mary that the shrine was to become a place for prayer, peace and atonement, as well as, redemption, grace and peace. But it has become much more.

Being the site of many miraculous photographs, the shrine of Our Lady of the Roses may be second only to Medjugorje in Miraculous Images. Many healings and other kinds of miracles have taken place at the shrine, too innumerable to mention.

Many of the messages that Veronica Leuken received included detailed visions of the Life and Death of Jesus Christ, the work and structure of Guardian Angels, and much information about the Holy Rosary and the Scapular of Our Lady of Mount Carmel.

And despite the death of Veronica Leuken in 1995, Our Lady promised that her presence would remain there until the time of the Second Coming of Christ

and many graces still come from this unusual shrine
in Bayside, New York.

Our Lady of Zeitoun, Egypt

One of the Few Mass Apparitions

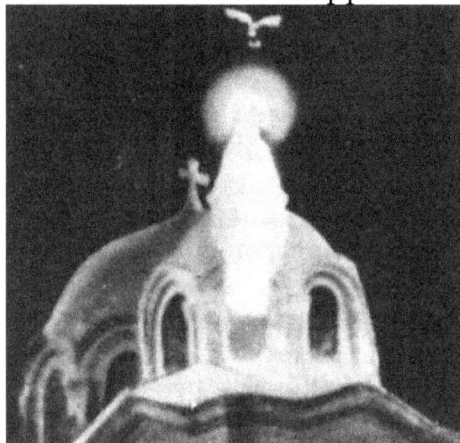

Our Lady of Zeitoun appeared to reportedly millions of people over a three year period beginning in 1968, much of it caught on film.

On April 2, 1968, a phenomenon that would take the world by storm began which would last a full three years. The Blessed Virgin began appearing over Cairo, Egypt in a manner that not only stunned the onlookers, all of whom could see her, but the filmmakers who were for the first time able to catch entire apparitions on film.

The Manifestation of Our Lady of Zeitoun, Egypt

The Blessed Mother appeared in many forms over the Coptic Orthodox Church which had been named in her honor. Rev. Constantine Moussa who has since passed, was the pastor of the church at the time of the apparitions. Apparitions of the Blessed Virgin Mary could last anywhere from five minutes to several hours.

Thousands of Egyptians witnessed the Blessed Virgin Mary clearly floating in the air above the church. Many of the apparitions were also noted to have accompanying luminous bodies around them, perhaps angels or heavenly messengers.

The apparitions were officially confirmed by His Holiness Pope Kyrillos VI (Cyril VI) who had entrusted a committee of high rank priests and bishops to investigate. Saturday, May 4, 1968, the apparitions were confirmed after in depth investigation.

Some are saying that the visits do continue until this day, just not as predicable.

The Message of Our Lady of Zietoun, Egypt

Our Lady of Zeitoun seems to carry a message of interesting import. As the Holy Family came into Egypt, legend tells us that all the Egyptian Pagan idols were instantly shattered and fell to the ground as a result of their mere presence.

The Holy Family traveled through many places in Egypt and did spend time near the location of the church in Cairo, Egypt. The Apparitions seem to be a commemoration of the journey of the Holy Family to Egypt – into the wilderness – and the mark that they left.

Other apparitions of interest include Our Lady of the Roses and Rosa Mystica, a unique apparition which seemed to be geared towards the clergy and not just the laypeople.

Rosa Mystica
The Mystical Rose

Mary appeared for the sole purpose of bringing her religious back to the heart of Jesus.

Occurring at Montichiari-Fontanelle, not far from the Lake Garda – a small little hamlet surrounded by huge mountain peaks and a town of about fourteen thousand people, the Blessed Virgin Mary came with a specific request for Pius XII.

The Manifestation of Rosa Mystica

Rosa Mystica – literally meaning Mystical Rose appeared to a young nurse, Pierina Gilli around 7 times, though no one knows the exact number. She came to Gilli wearing an beautiful white gown with a white veil over her head. She always carried a single pink rose in her hands.

The Message of Rosa Mystica

In the first apparition which occurred on December 8th of 1947, the Blessed Virgin Mary requested an hour of grace to be observed every 8th of December from that date forward.

The Holy Virgin handed Gilli three roses; yellow, white, and red in the second apparition saying that "The white rose represented the spirit of prayer, the red one represented the spirit of sacrifice, and the yellow rose the spirit of penance and conversion."

Because Gilli had not recognized who this apparition was, she asked *"Please tell me, who are you?"* She smiled and said, *"I am the Mother of Jesus and the Mother of all of you. Our Lord sends me to bring a new Marian Devotion to all religious orders and institutes, male and female, and to the priests of this world. I promise to protect those religious orders and institutes who will venerate me in this special way."*

When Pierina Gilli asked if a miracle would follow, the Blessed Virgin Mary replied in a different way from other apparitions. This message was for those leading a consecrated life, the religious. *"The religious who, for a long time now, have become indifferent thus betraying their vocation and as a result of their offenses have brought about the punishments and persecutions which are raging against the Church at the present time - will stop to offend Our Lord."*

It was Pope Pius VI who confirmed on November 21st, 1964, Mary, Mother of the Church.

Her messages could be summarized in these things: Prayer, Generous Sacrifices and Penance.

In her final messages after the date of her devotion had been set, the Blessed Virgin told Gilli that on December 8th at noon she would be in the Basilica and it would be an hour of great grace.

Sources

Those who Saw Her: Apparitions of Mary - Catherine M. Odell, *Catherine Laboure and the Modern Apparitions of Our Lady* - By Abbe Omer Englebert, *Miraculous Images: Photographs Containing God's Fingerprints* - By Marilynn Hughes, *Medjugorje: Light for the World* - By Pietro Jacopini, *Our Lady Comes to Garabandal* - By Joseph A. Pelletier, A.A., *The Wonder of Guadalupe* - By Francis Johnston, *The Glories of Czestochowa and Jasna, To the Priests Our Lady's Beloved Sons* - Marian Movement of Priests, *Our Lady of America* - By Sister Mildred Mary Neuzil, *The Thunder of Justice* - By Ted and Maureen Flynn

Marian Apparitions in the Catholic Church

An Overview
By Marilynn Hughes

The Out-of-Body Travel Foundation!

http://outofbodytravel.org

The Blessed Virgin Mary has been appearing throughout the centuries to a variety of people to give them messages of hope, prayer, penance and conversion. In this book, we cover thirty two of these Marian Apparitions to give you an overview of the events and messages of each one. This book gives you an overview and insight into a subject otherwise only understood through lengthy study.

Go to our Website at:

http://outofbodytravel.org

For more Information!

CPSIA information can be obtained
at www.ICGtesting.com
Printed in the USA
LVHW081253180219
607883LV00031B/552/P

9 781449 577025